LOVE

FULFILLING THE ULTIMATE QUEST

JAMES P. GILLS, M.D.

CREATION
HOUSE PRESS

LOVE: FULFILLING THE ULTIMATE QUEST
by James P. Gills, M.D.
Published by Creation House Press
A part of Strang Communications Company
600 Rinehart Road
Lake Mary, Florida 32746
www.creationhouse.com

Unless otherwise noted, Scripture quotations are from the King James version of the Bible. Used by permission.

Scripture quotations marked NASB are from the New American Standard Bible. Copyright © 1960, 1962, 1963, 1968, 1971, 1972, 1973, 1975, 1977 by the Lockman Foundation. Used by permission.

Scripture quotations marked AMP are from the Amplified Bible. Old Testament copyright © 1965, 1987 by the Zondervan Corporation. The Amplified New Testament copyright © 1954, 1958, 1987 by the Lockman Foundation. Used by permission.

Scripture quotations marked NIV are from the Holy Bible, New International Version. Copyright © 1973, 1978, 1984, International Bible Society. Used by permission of Zondervan Publishing House. All rights reserved.

Cover design by Judith McKittrick
Interior design by David Bilby

Library of Congress Control Number: 2002107032
International Standard Book Number: 0-88419-933-9
04 05 06 07—8 7 6 5 4 3 2
Printed in the United States of America

DEDICATION

To Shea and Pit,
Our two special children,
And to Shane and Joy,
Our son- and daughter-in-law.
And, to our grandchildren.
May you all learn to express the height and
depth of genuine love... better than I.
With deepest affection, and storge *(appreciation),*
Your dad.

ACKNOWLEDGMENTS

All praise goes to the Lord of Love
Who teaches us daily
To love others as He loves us.

Special thanks for the
Writing ministry of "HeartLight,"
And for Bud and Pat Hamm's
Service to our Savior
At Love Press

Love is the medicine for the sickness

of mankind. We can live

if we have love.

—Dr. Karl Menninger

The great tragedy of life is not that

men perish but that they

cease to love.

—W. SOMERSET MAUGHAM

CONTENTS

I believe in the sun even when it is not shining. I believe in love even when not feeling it. I believe in God even when He is silent.

PROLOGUE

One steamy June day in 1962 in south Georgia, a sixty-year-old Baptist minister with a pudgy frame and slow manner peered over his glasses at me. "Son," he asked, "why do you want to get married?"

What a stupid question! I thought. I searched for a fitting response, but visions of a beautiful, red-haired woman thrust aside any semblance of sanity. I could hardly wait for the charming Heather Rodgers to be my wife. She, too, anticipated the moment when I would be her handsome husband.

After an uneasy hesitation, I shrugged my shoulders. "We want to get married because...because we're in love."

He paused a few seconds. "What do you *mean* by love, Jim?"

He had me with that one. I shifted in my chair. The silence grew, but he wouldn't let me off the hook. Finally, trying to sound casual, I replied, "You know what I mean. We're just *in love*."

The kind, old reverend did not act the least bit surprised. He'd heard the same flimsy excuse for marriage many times over the years. He just smiled and proceeded to give me a few pointers. Since I'd been taught to respect my elders, I listened—as much as my youthful arrogance would allow.

I've contemplated love often since then and practiced it far less.

From what I read, I'm not alone in my struggles. Half of the marriages in the United States will end in a state of absolute *un-love*. It's called "divorce." (Now, we even have children who divorce their parents!) Few people I've met over the years—friends, colleagues, even ministers—claim to understand love, let alone know how to do it. I certainly had no idea when I got married. Romance, maybe. Love, no.

If "love makes the world go 'round," as the old song goes, then it's high time we discovered just what real love is. In this book, we'll examine this curious phenomenon under a high-powered, divine microscope to uncover its essential character. *What is love? What makes it grow healthy and strong? What kills it?* Together, let's probe for answers to these life-changing questions.

Why?

So we can love and be loved better than ever before!

What's so remarkable about love at first sight? It's when people have been looking at each other for years that it becomes remarkable.

PART ONE

~~~

LOVE AS WE KNOW IT

An Overview

There is no greater invitation to love

than in loving first.

At the ripe old age of twelve, I fell in love with a very attractive young lady who lived down the street. How I adored that girl! She was so pretty, and I sure liked kissing her. I didn't even mind getting my buck-teeth caught in her braces during those delightful moments. It didn't frustrate me one bit. That relationship fulfilled everything I really wanted out of love at that age. She made me look good and feel good, which did wonders for my ever-expanding, and fragile, male ego.

What was I *really* saying whenever I whispered, "I love you," to my pre-teen girlfriend? My bold statements said, "I love *myself.* I just want you to help me do it."

We're all the same. It's a matter of degree. Our expressions of love (too often shaped by the sales-conscious media), bear a striking resemblance to what I experienced at that tender age. Perhaps, where love is concerned, it's time we left our skate keys and teddy bears behind. My goal, through this book, is to help us *(including myself)* do just that.

Children engage in lots of fuzzy thinking and speaking, but what about adults? We intellectuals use the same four-letter word to describe the way we feel about a vast assortment of topics. I love my wife. I love my children. I love my dog. I love my profession. I love ice cream. I love windsurfing. I love, I love, I love. And in the same breath, we exclaim, "I love God, and He loves me!" No wonder we're confused!

The ancient Greeks were more specific. They used five different words for various types of love: *epithumia, eros, philia, storge* and *agape.* However, that list seems a bit

Love seeketh not itself to please,

Nor for itself hath any care,

But for another gives its ease,

And builds a Heaven

in Hell's despair.

—WILLIAM BLAKE

cumbersome to remember. Over my years of studying the Bible, two other concepts of love have emerged in my mind. I've taken the liberty of adding them as the sixth and seventh types. In essence, they *summarize* the dynamics of love from one end of the spectrum to the other.

Let's call the sixth form, *selfishness*, and the seventh, *commitment*. Some scholars say that six is the Hebrew number for man because God created man on the sixth day. Given man's addiction to self, making selfishness sixth on the list seems appropriate. Seven represents fullness, or perfection, since God rested on the seventh day after completing the task of creation. So, designating commitment as the seventh type of love associates it with our goal—perfected love. Much of this book will focus on these last two, but before we delve into deeper waters, let's spend a minute on the five types of love, according to the Greeks.

Epithumia is translated as desire, earnest desire, impulse, and lust. In the Bible it is used in both its positive and negative senses. For example, Jesus said, "I have *earnestly desired* to eat this Passover with you before I suffer" (Luke 22:15). Within the context of marriage, the Bible sanctions the healthy need couples have to unite sexually. Fulfilling normal physical desires should provide them with many hours of mutual enjoyment, and encourage them to be fruitful and multiply.

On the other hand, we also see the negative, distorted side of *epithumia,* which is a passionate desire for forbidden pleasure. "Let not sin therefore reign in your mortal body, that you should obey it in the lusts thereof" (Rom. 6:12). Outside of marriage, uncontrolled *epithumia* devastates individuals and society. To Aristotle, it meant groping for pleasure. Clement of Alexandria said about the same, referring to it as an unreasonable craving for gratification.

I have found the paradox that if I

love until it hurts, then there is not

hurt, but only more love.

—MOTHER TERESA
OF CALCUTTA

The ancient Stoics defined *epithumia* as a reaching after pleasure which defied all reason.

When a man chooses this way of life and immerses himself in the world, he ceases to be aware of God at all. Perverted desire can exert so much power over men's minds that they do outrageous, "nameless and shameless" things. Modern psychology says an addiction has taken root. The "love object" consumes and controls them.

Next comes *eros*, a familiar term to many in the list of the five Greek types of love. Sensual, erotic messages abound these days. One can hardly miss the countless advertisements that play on this aspect of human nature. Please don't misunderstand, though. Romantic infatuation can be a beautiful experience. (Cupid still gets the credit for shooting his arrow into unsuspecting hearts.) Think back to that first crush you had as a youth. For some of us, that may take us back quite a while, so take a moment to reminisce. Enjoy the memories.

Do you remember how you felt whenever you saw that person, or even just thought about him or her? A warm "rush" inside moved you in a way very little else could, and that's good. Fresh and pure, lofty and noble, *eros* can stir us on to new heights of love. Without it, none of us would even be here, and few of us care to live without it. Scripture supports us in our feelings.

Eros holds a special place in a married couple's life together, as the Song of Solomon brings to our attention. Mutual love, expressed so tenderly between the shepherd and his new wife, teaches us not to scorn, but to appreciate, romantic passion. God places His stamp of approval on the act of lovemaking. How could we despise a gift God has given us? His Word tells us that "every good and perfect gift is from above" (James 1:17, NIV).

The Song of Solomon presents quite a case against an

His love enableth me to call every

country my country, and every

man my brother.

—DANIEL WHEELER

unbiblical separation between the physical, emotional and spiritual relationships within a marriage. This loving couple sets a good example for us to follow. We, too, can achieve a beautiful union of the physical and spiritual during intimate moments. Consider the time a celebration.

I believe God would be delighted if we thanked Him for our mates and prayed together during intimacy. It would add a whole new dimension to our relationships.

Philia brings to mind a different kind of love altogether. Have you ever wondered how Philadelphia acquired the name, "city of brotherly love"? I'll give you a clue. Whether or not friendly folks live there, the root word, *philia*, refers to friendship—the warm affection between girlfriends, buddies, pals, comrades, chums. Hence, Philadelphia's nickname. The word *philos* occurs 188 times in the Bible, and most of those translate directly as "friend." It never refers to God's love for man or man's love for God. Where we think of *eros* as a private passion, *philia* is a public friendship. Developed over time, it can bless both parties to the utmost.

We find one of Scripture's better-known examples of *philia* in the friendship that blossomed between Jonathan and David. The son of Israel's first king, Saul, and the one who would become Israel's greatest king, grew to love one another as brothers. We read in 1 Samuel 18:1, 3:

> And it came to pass, when he had made an end of speaking unto Saul, that the soul of Jonathan was knit with the soul of David…Then Jonathan and David made a covenant, because he loved him as his own soul.

James, in his epistle, gives a word of caution concerning friendships. Not every opportunity to develop such closeness benefits a Christian; some friends hinder our relationship

Faith is the key to fit the door of hope, but there is no power anywhere like love for turning it.

—ELAINE EMANS

with God. People following the world's way of doing things have different priorities from those who strive to follow Jesus. James 4:4 states that friendship with the world means enmity (animosity, hostility) against God. That doesn't give us the right to walk around with our noses up in the air, unwilling to extend our hands to those around us. We're here to minister, but we're not to get ensnared in any relationship which places us at odds with God.

Storge, the fourth type of love, can best be described as good, old-fashioned family love, or an appreciative fondness. That almost indestructible bond between parents and their children overcomes terrible obstacles. It endures for a lifetime. And where this type of love abounds, a unique freedom exists to experience life, with all its joys and sorrows.

Many times, we learn life's lessons by living. A loving home environment helps. Parents teach children sound biblical principles of right and wrong, of course, and prepare them to survive those difficult lessons. *Storge* doesn't burden or oppress the young into bondage. Like a mother eagle with her brood of eaglets, *storge* encourages children to stretch out and test their wings. It doesn't isolate them from the reality of life, and if, after all the teaching, they still yearn to set out on their own course, *storge* allows them that freedom—when they have come of age and can fend for themselves.

The parable of the prodigal son, found in the fifteenth chapter of Luke, illustrates *storge* at work. When the son demanded his share of the inheritance, the father gave it to him. With a heavy heart (and what father's heart wouldn't be heavy?), he allowed him to go. Later, when the son returned home, defeated, we see the beauty of a family enduring one of life's bitter lessons. They suffered from the son's wayward days, but in the end, what better illustration

The world is full of beauty when

your heart is filled with love.

could the Lord have used to depict our heavenly Father's "familial" love for all returning prodigals?

> And the son said unto him, Father, I have sinned against heaven, and in thy sight, and am no more worthy to be called thy son. But the father said to his servants, Bring forth the best robe, and put it on him; and put a ring on his hand, and shoes on his feet...For this my son was dead and is alive again.
>
> —LUKE 15:21, 22, 24

Agape, giving of yourself without yielding to a "What's-in-it-for-me?" attitude, best describes the fifth type of love. Only God specializes in *agape*, a devotion that gives whatever is best for others without thought of self-gain.

In one of my books, *Come Unto Me*, I spoke about God's commission to Moses from the burning bush. Israel had cried for deliverance from Egyptian slavery and stirred God's heart of compassion. So moved, and when the time was right, He sent Moses. Did the people want him? Not a chance. They yearned for an immediate, miraculous deliverance, but God knew what they *needed*.

Our own wants and needs don't line up sometimes, either, do they? God knows the end from the beginning, so He gives what the situation calls for—nothing more, and nothing less. *Agape* love does that. It desires to accomplish the best results, without thought of cost to self. Moses responded to God's call with *agape* love. He abandoned a lavish lifestyle in the royal courts of Egypt to save his countrymen.

Several thousand years later, the Jews were once again crying out for someone to liberate them from oppression—this time at the hands of the Romans. In the fullness of time, God the Father sent such a Deliverer to the Israelites. Jesus

It is hard to express love

with a clenched fist.

didn't fit the description of the king they had in mind, either; but they needed Him. Jesus came to restore mankind, including the Romans, to fellowship with God. He came to pay the full penalty for sin, not just to rescue people from one bad situation so they could fall into another. Salvation cost Him everything.

Since *agape* is God's kind of love, and thus unique, we'll devote a section to it in Part Three of the book. We'll look at the many faces of *agape* and how to make it real in all our relationships. First, a quick peek at that old enemy— love of self. It stops divine love in its tracks.

None of us ever attends a School of Selfishness, yet even as newborn babies, we demonstrate great skill in this area. Without effort, I might add! Infants reach out, clenching their tiny hands around whatever they can grab.

Ambitious youngsters take whatever they want to amuse them at the moment.

Piaget, a well-known child development specialist, explains the natural growth process. He talks about the cycle of selfishness, and says that it surfaces at the mother's breast. As children progress from those early days on through adulthood, ideally, they become less dependent and more responsible, less demanding and more giving. The boy who takes should mature into the father who gives; the self-absorbed girl should blossom into a child-centered mother.

Young ladies who grow up conscious of their charm and beauty often make many demands. They select a husband based on his ability to meet these demands, and they get most of what they want from him. Then, a surprise arrives— a baby! This new addition forces some change from self-centeredness to selflessness. Rather than being waited upon, the mother projects her needs and wants onto the child. Not all mothers, however, readily accept the new routine. Some

This heartwarming ad appeared in the classified section of a dignified metropolitan paper:

"I am responsible for all debts and obligations of my wife, Julia, both present and future, and am delighted to be the provider for a woman who has borne me two fine children, listened patiently to all my gripes, and with an overabundance of love and care made the past fifteen years of my life the happiest I have known. On this our fifteenth wedding anniversary, I am proud to express my gratitude publicly."

young women have become so accustomed to getting the attention themselves, they cannot stand being out of the limelight. They never learn how to give. The change from selfishness to selflessness is indeed, difficult and unbearable for some.

Others find motherhood the most fulfilling time in their lives as they overflow with the love of God. A closeness beyond all boundaries unites a woman with her baby, who is dependent upon her for its survival, and who will always be "her child." Of course, the recipient of the 3:00 A.M. feeding never notices her pink satin boudoir slippers. The cycle has come full circle as the perfumed, pampered lover becomes a baby-scented, pampering mother.

To some extent, customs, laws and cultural pressure do curb a selfish attitude of "I want, therefore I'll take." But unless a radical spiritual transformation occurs, we'll never grow to adopt a motto of, "I live, therefore, I'll give." Fallen human nature, even motivated by good intentions, cannot produce perfect *agape*.

I discovered a word that describes what must occur before even a hint of *agape* can emerge through our human vessels: *metanoia*. No, not paranoia. *Metanoia*: A radical change in thinking. It's related to another word many of us have heard a time or two: metamorphosis—the type of transformation that turns a caterpillar into a butterfly. And it means more than just a slight departure from the usual. Metanoia involves a drastic, about-face type of change in thought.

One reason for such a radial change lies in the insidious nature of the sixth type of love. Selfishness, cunning and deceitful, would rather join forces with one of the other five types of love and pervert their essential goodness, than stand alone. Selfishness acts like a *cancer* of love. We usually see it stirring its ugly head under the

Commitment gives substance to love.

—Heather Gills

guise of self-preservation. It can grow to such an extent that people dedicate their entire existence to a struggle for recognition and self-fulfillment.

The world glamorizes taking care of self first. Whenever we focus our goals on personal achievements, affluent living conditions and physical satisfaction, we destroy all hope of ever experiencing the meaningful love God intends for His children to have. Shallow, immature Madison Avenue love barely skims the surface.

Once we understand *agape*, most of us find it an impossible task. A consuming love of self prohibits our surrendering completely to God's will. We might be able to fool one another for a time, and even convince ourselves that we've got everything under control; but sooner or later our selfish nature prevails. Up it springs, if not in the same area, then in another.

Marriage does not do away with the danger. It simply exposes the truth. Young people often jump into marriage for what they can enjoy rather than what they can contribute. What a setup for disaster! Jonathan Edwards, a prolific writer and pastor of the 1700s, wrote in his book, *Charity and Its Fruits*, about self-love and the result of Adam's sin. His language may sound a bit stuffy, but his observations and imagery remain quite contemporary:

> The ruin that the fall brought upon the soul of man consists very much in his losing the nobler and more benevolent principles of his nature, and falling wholly under the power and government of self-love...Before, his soul was under the government of that noble principle of divine love, whereby it was enlarged to the comprehension of all his fellow-creatures and their welfare...But so soon as he had transgressed against God, these nobler principles

Love is only for the young,

the middle-aged, and the old.

were immediately lost, and all this excellent enlarged-ness of man's soul was gone; and thenceforward he himself shrank, as it were, into a little space, circum-scribed and closely shut up within itself, to the exclu-sion of all things else." (pp. 157–158).

That brings me to a brief look at the opposite end of the spectrum, to *commitment*, the seventh type of love. We'll delve into this very important subject in greater depth later in the book, also. When you get right down to it, com-mitment represents the ultimate form of selflessness. It makes us more willing and able to sacrifice for others.

A strong foundation of commitment must be laid before the wedding vows if we expect them to stick after the hon-eymoon. Compare the playboy who gets engaged and still goes out on his fiancée, to a young woman in our neigh-borhood. She realized one day she had found the man she should marry. Without any great fanfare, she quit dating anyone else. During their courtship, she supported and encouraged him, and after marriage, her commitment remained strong. Even though he had some setbacks, she never allowed anyone to ridicule him. She helped make him into the very best of men because she recognized her husband as the man God had sent to her.

I can remember growing up in my hometown with dreams of a special someone to love, so I could find fulfill-ment as a man. To my surprise, I discovered I had to *com-mit* myself to one woman (and eliminate all my other options). By a contract ordained in heaven, she was to be special, both to Him and to me. If that didn't confuse a man of my tender years and little spiritual revelation, I also sought significance through my profession.

Looking back, I can see that I really needed the Lord.

He had given Himself to me; I only had to commit myself and my love to Him. Had I done so, the rest of my desires would have fallen into place. Instead, I intellectualized, humanized and rationalized my way out of obligation to anyone but myself. I even studied existential theology, trying to find a loophole.

This persisted for years. I kept Jesus at bay, at what I thought was a safe distance, and refused His offer of divine intimacy. Finally, I discovered the real Christian life. All my efforts at finding myself and my special niche only kept me away from the One I needed most. I found the answer I'd been searching for in His love. You can, too—if you get honest with yourself and Him. I'll explain more in Part Two.

The happiest mind is the mind

that cares for others.

PART TWO

~~~

LOVE AT ITS WORST

Selfishness Up Close

Love is the only force capable of

transforming an enemy

into a friend.

—MARTIN LUTHER KING, JR.

Greece said, "Be wise—know yourself." Rome said, "Be strong—discipline yourself." Psychology says, "Be confident—assert yourself." Materialism says, "Be satisfied—please yourself." Religion says, "Be good—conform yourself."

I tried all that advice over the years and it left me empty. Jesus said, "Deny yourself and follow Me" (Matt. 16:24).

I'm learning, one day at a time.

How *do* we become more concerned for others and less so for our own comfort? First, we have one thing to unlearn. Despite current philosophies, we *can* survive (and thrive) without our addiction to self.

William Booth, founder of the Salvation Army, said, "The most important word is *others*." Mother Teresa of Calcutta had the same idea. She said, "Life is not worth living unless it is lived for others." As she ministered to outcast lepers in India, she exemplified the mature, balanced Christian walk. Those poor people could not help themselves, and could do nothing for her in return. What a high ideal she set! She fulfilled the command in Scripture, "Be kindly affectioned one to another with brotherly love; in honor preferring one another" (Rom. 12:10).

Superficial Christianity pops up everywhere. People perform according to preconceived notions and mimic what they believe a Christian should be. Such lifestyles produce only temporary satisfaction and double standards. During this shallow period in my own life, how did I act? I studied

It seems to be our destiny never to love anything without seeking to alter it, and in altering it to make it other than what we first loved.

the Word. I attended retreats. I even taught Sunday school! But surrender my whole self to the Lord? Far from it.

Before I learned the value of genuine commitment, I was nothing more than a "cosmetic Christian." My religion went skin deep. Oh, I had been born-again years before, but I had no burning desire to love or obey God. Now I know the difference. I may fail at times to practice what I believe, but I *want to*. At least I'm learning to trust the Lord instead of myself to make it happen. As a more dedicated Christian, I still find myself torn between *devotion to me* and *devotion to Him*. The apostle Paul spoke of a similar struggle: "For I have the desire to do what is good, but I cannot carry it out. For what I do is not the good I want to do; no, the evil I do not want to do—this I keep on doing" (Rom. 7:18b,19, NIV).

Ingrained selfish habits can so overwhelm us that any victory seems an insurmountable task. And yet, we must strive to win the battle. So much lies at stake—for us and the world.

According to many experts in human behavior, selfishness stands alone as the most common mental illness. O. Quentin Hyden, M.D., supports this concept in his book, *A Christian's Handbook of Psychiatry*:

> Selfishness is the root cause of all sin, and the result of sin may sometimes lead to personality or adjustment problems and some neurotic, psychosomatic or even psychotic conditions.

Of course, Dr. Hyden assures us that sin alone doesn't cause *all* mental breakdowns or emotional disturbances, but it plays a key role. We could presume, then, that the opposite is also true. The soundest state of mind—in an individual or a nation—is selflessness. OK. Forget the fifty

Love at first sight usually ends

with divorce at first slight.

dollar words and remember this: for sound mental health, develop the desire to *give* rather than *take*.

In case we lack the motivation to conquer our old foe, a short tour through history might provide the incentive. Ancient Rome, that vast and mighty civilization, fell prey to pagan enemies. First, though, it fell prey to the enemy within. The core rotted. Selfishness enjoyed a heyday. Leaders and followers alike cared more about their own pleasure than anything else. We need only to look around at our beloved America to see many of the same tendencies. We're rushing down the path at breakneck speed. Without major changes, we may very well wind up suffering the same fate—or worse. Noted author and speaker, Chuck Colson, said in a recent message, "The greatest crisis in America today is the crisis of character...no society has ever survived without a strong moral code." Sobering words, indeed.

Selfish hindrances, like litter strewn beside a scenic highway, mar the landscape along the road to God's kind of love. It spoils the trip. A greater awareness of specific "me-isms" helps us detect them—and dispose of them. Do any of the following habits sound familiar? Worry, self-pity, manipulation and greed, to name but a few.

As I see it, selfishness and cataracts have a lot in common. (Maybe that's because I've been an eye surgeon for over thirty years.) Cataracts restrict physical sight; selfishness obstructs spiritual sight. I've removed many cloudy lenses and implanted brand new ones, enabling light to focus on the retina so people can see.

"Spiritual cataracts," in whatever form, darken our hearts and minds. They hinder the radiant light of Christ's love from shining through us to the world. It takes more than a phacoemulsifier machine to remove the stubborn

The world crowns success,

but God crowns faithfulness!

spiritual kind of cataract—only the divine Physician has the necessary skill and tools to do that. If you're ready, let Him begin the examination.

Selfishness Goes to School

In Psalm 118:8, we read, "It is better to trust in the LORD than to put confidence in man." Humanism tries to transform selfishness into "science." One of its basic tenets declares that we must love ourselves before we can love anyone else. Christians believe otherwise. Not only does humanism attempt to remove God from the "love loop," it elevates man above God. In practical experience, the concept proves false.

People do not love others better by loving themselves more; they only grow into more proficient narcissists. These psychological theories, and various other forms of counseling, deviate from the teachings of Scripture. "Self-realization" and "finding yourself" have attained a measure of popularity among humanists, but the methods they use to achieve their goals lead to the enthronement of work and personal accomplishments. What a contrast to the saint who enthrones Jesus Christ in all he does!

The "What-Ifs" Syndrome

Did you ever think of worry as a kind of faith? It is. Faith in Satan instead of in God! Why is worry selfish? It forces us to fixate on, and fret about, potential harm to *self* (or others important to self). It negates faith in God's promises. Worry can devastate a person's health. Not only that, it can spread to others close to us, like an unseen, contagious disease. In an earlier book, *Come Unto Me*, I listed

Humility is a strange thing—

when you think you've gained it,

you've lost it.

eighteen thoughts from *Dake's Annotated Reference Bible* about this first-cousin to self-pity. Reverend Dake did such an outstanding job, I've included the list once again.

Worry is:
1. Sinful and produced by fear.
2. A disease causing other ills.
3. Borrowing trouble that cannot be paid back.
4. Brooding over what may not happen.
5. Creating trouble, misery and death.
6. A burden borrowed from time or others.
7. Weight that kills prematurely.
8. Mental and physical suicide.
9. A gravedigger that has no sympathy.
10. Needless and wasted time and effort that should be spent constructively.
11. A robber of faith, peace and trust in an never-failing heavenly Father.
12. A stumbling block to others.
13. A disgrace to God that should never be indulged in by Christians.
14. Anxiety over what is nothing today and what is less tomorrow, in view of faith.
15. Anticipating troubles which seldom come to those who trust God.
16. Torment over something that will likely be a blessing if it comes.
17. Living like an orphan without a heavenly Father.
18. A crime against God, man, nature and better judgment. *Jehovah Shalom* is God's peace in righteousness.

—DAKE NEW TESTAMENT (P. 6)

Whenever I waste time stewing about legal, family or

He who lives only for himself

is truly dead to others.

—Publilius Syrus

business matters, I wind up in an emotional cauldron. Worry reduces my effectiveness and restricts my capacity for love. I can't detect the needs of others around me while my thoughts churn away on personal concerns.

Does worry about others, especially our children, mean we love them more? Not at all. In fact, it means we like to court sin. We can't get away with worry if we line it up against the Word. (See Matthew 6:25–34; Luke 12:29 and Philippians 4:19.) Here's one of my favorite Scriptures to memorize:

> Be anxious for nothing, but in everything by prayer and supplication with thanksgiving let your requests be made known to God. And the peace of God, which surpasses all comprehension, shall guard your hearts and your minds in Christ Jesus.
>
> —Philippians 4:6, nasb

Pity Parties Are for Kids

Self-pity ranks high on the selfishness scale. It grieves God. If you doubt that, turn to the book of Numbers and read the story of the Israelites who murmured while trekking through the wilderness. A "poor-me" attitude focuses on unfulfilled personal wants, leaving no room to thank God for His many blessings. (See 1 Timothy 6:6 and Philippians 4:11.)

Legitimate feelings of self-concern have their place. Even Jesus expressed these emotions. (Read His prayer in the Garden of Gethsemane the night before His crucifixion in Mark 14:32–36.) Our complaints, in contrast to His, usually stem from ingratitude, worry and self-condemnation more than from any righteous cause.

The "normal" self-pity found in young children should change as they mature. Often, that doesn't happen.

The need for devotion to something outside ourselves is even more profound than the need for companionship. If we are not to go to pieces or wither away, we all must have some purpose in life; for no man can live for himself alone.

—Ross Parmenter

Children grow up physically, yet fail to attain any level of spiritual maturity. As a result, they develop negative attitudes toward everything in life.

We've all dealt with adults who forever whine about their circumstances—from their deficient wardrobes and physical attributes to their mates, friends, houses, churches, jobs...Approximately seventy-five percent of American workers dislike their jobs—many enough to criticize them at length with anyone who will listen.

As a rule, people who wallow in self-pity make unrealistic appraisals of life. For example, some workers expect to receive higher wages without giving anything of value in exchange. This type of attitude infects others around them and saps their strength. As a wise man of old wrote, "A merry heart doeth good like a medicine: but a broken spirit drieth the bones" (Prov. 17:22).

I would venture to guess that most of us succumb to self-pity now and then. Some days I really indulge myself, when everything doesn't go my way or when associates don't "cater" to me enough. At the clinic, I sometimes have to repeat instructions over and over. Nobody listens to me. My throat gets sore, and I start feeling sorry for myself. My attitude takes a big turn for the worse.

While I'm wallowing in the mire, I forget others' needs. Many people, especially senior citizens, may simply have a hard time hearing me! I've since found a logical solution for the dilemma: I encourage my staff to share the responsibility of giving important instructions.

The art of contentment takes time, but if we are to demonstrate God's love, we will expend the effort. Without whining. "Not that I speak in respect of want: for I have learned, in whatsoever state I am, therewith to be content" (Phil. 4:11).

Love looks through a telescope;

envy, through a microscope.

Losing the Blame Game

The awareness of wrongs we've committed in the past hangs over our heads like a heavy weight. We don't know quite when the load will drop and crush us. Guilt gnaws on our innards like a swarm of termites on a piece of choice wood, until we're left feeling hollow and worthless.

When that happens, it's a safe bet we're not living under the grace of God. In that risky condition, we can never relax enough to love Him, people or life. But, oh, when we come to Jesus! God shows His deep love for us through the gift of forgiveness. He releases us from the threatening burden of sin and guilt.

I remember the sense of relief that flooded my soul the day I accepted Jesus as Lord, and I often see similar relief mirrored in others with new faith. His peace far outperforms any anti-depressant on the market. As John 14:27 says, "Peace I leave with you, my peace I give unto you: not as the world giveth, give I unto you. Let not your heart be troubled, neither let it be afraid."

The Holy Spirit does convince us of sin by making us uncomfortable until we admit it, but we shouldn't confuse that with a nagging feeling called *false guilt*. Godly conviction leads us to repentance and back to God, while false guilt drives a wedge between us and Him.

For example, an adult who was molested as a child carries inside a "shame core" for a sin not his to claim. Or, consider the many believers who ask for forgiveness over and over for the same sin because they harbor false guilt.

"Then how can guilt ever be selfish?" you might wonder. Consider this: clinging to guilt involves a decision to place self (personal ego/feelings) on the throne instead of God's Word. He says if we admit sin with a sincere heart,

Discipline puts back in its place

that something in us

which should serve

but wants to rule.

　　　　　—A. Carthusian

He will forgive. He will bind up our wounds. He will set us free. End of guilt! Out of pride, we say, "I'd rather not confess to God or anyone else, thank you. I prefer to stay miserable in my sin."

True contentment thrives only in the fertile hearts of those who know they have been forgiven. Daily, we need to ask for and receive that forgiveness so we can forget the past and look forward to the joy of being with Him forever. Why wait 'til forever? Do it now. "If we confess our sins, he is faithful and just to forgive us our sins, and to cleanse us from all unrighteousness" (1 John 1:9, NIV).

The Greener-Grass Trap

According to Greek legend, a prominent athlete placed second in an important race. He brooded over his loss night and day. Envy consumed him—so much, that he decided to destroy a large statue erected in the winner's honor. As he chopped at its base, the statue fell and crushed him. What a lesson for us!

Nothing can appease a selfish heart full of envy. If it cannot overtake the one envied on its own merits, it will surely try to rob the achievements, possessions or blessings of that person. Things get out of hand when this vile emotion runs wild.

Many biblical stories warn us of the danger of envy. The sibling rivalry between Cain and Abel festered and caused Cain to kill his brother. Joseph's jealous brothers seized the opportunity to sell him into foreign slavery. King Saul envied David to the point of madness and attempted murder. Even mature Christians who yield to a lesser degree of envy cut off intimacy with God and others. "Let us not be desirous of vain glory, provoking one another,

Loves does not dominate;

it cultivates.

—GOETHE

envying one another" (Gal. 5:26). "But put ye on the Lord Jesus Christ…" (Rom. 13:14a).

NOT-SO-WISER MISERS

Selfish greed mixed with fear produces imbalances, improper evaluations and poor decision-making. A quick glance at the stock market provides a good example in the business world. It is understood that greed can cause swings in the stock market. Investors rush to buy huge amounts of a particular company's stock, forcing the price up. Then, fearful of incurring losses, they sell their shares and decrease the value significantly for everyone. This allows them to buy back at even lower prices.

In relationships, a similar cycle appears. A selfish person, concerned only with immediate gratification, will "buy into" a relationship for what he or she can get out of it. Then, rather than becoming vulnerable enough to develop mutual trust and love, fear of rejection (loss) forces flight to the next "quick-gain" affair. If we commit our whole selves to God, this destructive fear-producing cycle will not plague us, either in business or in personal relationships. We rest in His unconditional love, so we can risk loving others. "There is no fear in love; but perfect love casteth out fear" (1 John 4:18).

DOMINATION STATION

Do you know anyone suffering from eating disorders like bulimia or anorexia nervosa? For whatever emotional reasons, the victims of such disorders have a high need to control something in their lives, so they choose the most accessible thing—their bodies. They manipulate dietary

Some pray to marry the man they love,

My prayers will somewhat vary:

I humbly pray to Heaven above

that I love the man I marry.

—ROSE STOKES

habits to the point of self-destruction.

The same thing can happen in interpersonal relation-ships. Whether within the family, church or business com-munity, everyone suffers when we direct others for our own selfish gain (under the guise of having their best inter-est at heart). Even if we temporarily succeed in getting our way, bitterness takes root in those we treat this way. They may not even know why they feel animosity, but uncon-sciously they know they've been used. They resent it.

A manipulator neither appreciates nor respects others. To him, people are objects to do with as he pleases. This opposes the gentle Holy Spirit, who values every creature and never forces Himself on anyone.

Those who selfishly manipulate others worry most about being in charge and about who's "calling the shots." Issues such as a sudden financial setback, loss of position or death create a special anxiety. Why? Because all these sit-uations leave us with zero control. We can combat these feelings in the area of finances by becoming good stewards over what we have: giving a generous portion of our income to charity and committing the remainder to God.

The Lord supplies everything we obtain in life—youthfulness, health, possessions or family. Someday, whether we want to or not, we must release it all to Him anyway. Choosing to do this now, in the name of the Lord, exemplifies the highest kind of love. It also lets us be whole and free. "Delight thyself in the Lord, and do good; so shalt thou dwell in the land, and verily thou shalt be fed. Delight thyself also in the Lord; and He shall give thee the desires of thine heart" (Ps. 37:5).

The level of lust parallels the level of selfishness. The level of commitment parallels the level of love.

—JIM GILLS

"What's Yours Is Mine"

In America, when a company catches an employee stealing (whether outright or through poor work habits), they will probably not retain that employee's services any longer. He has broken trust and destroyed his credibility.

Americans have occasionally watched national news in shock as looters took advantage of victims' misfortune during storms or riots. They walked into broken-down store fronts and homes to carry off whatever they could use.

In some cultures, people "make ends meet," not by working hard, but by stealing. Once headed down such a path, they soon convince themselves of their dependence upon thievery to survive. These people get trapped in a deteriorating physical and spiritual ghetto. We read in Galatians 6:7–8:

> Be not deceived; God is not mocked: for whatsoever a man soweth, that shall he also reap. For he that soweth to his flesh shall of the flesh reap corruption; but he that soweth to the Spirit shall of the Spirit reap life everlasting.

The thief has a hard time loving God or his fellow man, but Jesus can transform his life from one of taking to one of giving. God is love, and love gives. "For God so loved the world, that He gave his only begotten Son…" (John 3:16).

"Story" Hour

A young wife goes on a shopping spree and spends five hundred dollars. Knowing the family is tight for money, she tells her husband she spent one hundred dollars. A new business in town expands quickly because the owner has a

Don't look down on anyone;

only God sits that high.

special knack with customers. His competitors spread rumors that he's on the verge of bankruptcy.

Advantages finagled through lies, either "white" or black, always result in reduced rewards in the end. This selfish habit, used to protect oneself by altering the truth, or to destroy another's credibility, ends up damaging the perpetrator. It colors every contact from then on.

Love demands truthfulness, even when it hurts. Ephesians 4:15 in the Amplified Bible says, "let our lives lovingly express truth in all things—speaking truly, dealing truly, living truly." Proverbs 18:21 reminds us, "Death and life are in the power of the tongue; and they that love it shall eat the fruit thereof."

Longing for Forbidden Fruit

From the moment we learn to reason until the time we die, we all struggle with lust. It comes in various forms (for food, possessions, power, etc.) and degrees (even to the point of addiction), but we hear most about sexual lust—the counterfeit of marital love.

We do not have to commit an act of adultery to open the door to destruction. Mental adultery works the same way. It tears us away from the peace of God-directed love and unity in marriage. In place of a beautiful gift, it offers only frustration and loneliness.

I fell prey to such deception early in my married life when I read *Playboy* magazines. Although considered tame by today's standards, in the light of Scripture they are still pornographic. Reading them led me to wonder whether my marital relationship lacked something. They fed the selfish side of me that placed my own pleasure above my marriage.

Selfishness prompts all sexual relationships outside the

The loneliest place in the world

is the human heart when

love is absent.

—E. C. McKenzie

bonds of marriage. Giving in to such desires inflicts painful soul wounds that remain long after the activity stops or the partners marry. Oh, if they confess the sin, God will forgive them; but the consequences of a few moments of stolen pleasure can last a lifetime.

Adulterous desires leave us when we discover the satisfaction that only comes through a life of commitment. Couples in harmony with the Lord's will, remember they *belong* to him. As my devotion to both the Lord and Heather has grown, I've long since realized that pornography misses the mark. I'm so thankful that I discovered the joy of a committed love to Jesus and to my lovely wife.

God's way fulfills us more than premarital or extramarital sex ever could, simply because it is His best. When we have the best, who wants the rest? Overcoming mental lust within marriage, however, still requires work. I have found that an intimate prayer life with my wife helps remove some past barriers to deeper intimacy.

"Let your fountain [of human life] be blessed [with the rewards of fidelity], and rejoice with the wife of your youth" (Prov. 5:18, AMP).

UPPITY YUPPITIES

Any time we look down on other people and focus only on their weak points, we reveal our own self-righteous pride. We use the technique for a purpose—to draw attention away from our inadequacy and insecurity. It protects self from close-up scrutiny and, therefore, hinders intimate communication. All this convinces us that we still reign at the center of our own little worlds. From such a lofty position of self-deception, we make unwise decisions with serious consequences. As it says in Proverbs

Love begins when a person feels another person's needs are as important as his own.

—SULLIVAN

16:18, "Pride goeth before destruction, and an haughty spirit before a fall."

No Different Strokes for Different Folks

Our investment corporation, Jireh, employs two opposite types of people—accountants and developers. The developers do manage to get investments done, but the accountants don't appreciate their "super-optimism" one bit. They tend to believe what Arthur James Balfour said (with tongue in cheek): "It is unfortunate, considering enthusiasm moves the world, that so few enthusiasts can be trusted to speak the truth." Not to be outdone, the developers show little patience for the accountants' seeming inability to move on an idea.

Even though people with these different personalities have always had to work hard to understand each other, we need the stability they provide in business and elsewhere. In church, the "doers" (developers, positive thinkers, enthusiasts) will try almost anything to become more effective for Jesus. The "thinkers" (accountants, planners and realists) frown on these free spirits. The former emphasize prayer and Bible study to the exclusion of reaching out. All the varied mentalities have their special niche in a Christian-centered balance of truth and progress.

I have seen churches where differing ideas flourish like wildflowers in a beautiful meadow. In other congregations, members stumble over mundane details, like what color the new carpet and choir robes should be. Selfish, petty differences lead to serious strife—on a local and national scale. Families leave and some churches even split apart because

The person who is always finding

fault, seldom finds anything else.

people refuse to appreciate each others' uniquenesses and opinions. Instead, they open the door to severe criticism.

Conflict will arise in every relationship, whether it's a large group or two mates. Judson Edwards describes the problem well in his book, *What They Never Told Us About How to Get Along With Each Other*. He mentions that relationships are like collisions of different worlds; we just need to make them *tender collisions*.

Tender collisions bring up the image of a friendly round of bumper cars at the county fair—in contrast to a bad accident on the interstate. Which would we prefer? We can disagree, but in healthy relationships, we decide to walk in love and let the final authority rest on the Word of God. As a wise man said, "Major in majors and minor in minors."

The apostle Paul admonishes us: "With all lowliness and meekness, with long-suffering forbearing one another in love, endeavouring to keep the unity of the Spirit in the bond of peace" (Eph. 4:2–3).

DON'T CONFUSE ME WITH FACTS ... MY MIND IS MADE UP

Unbelief could adopt that phrase as its slogan. In fact, unbelief is the epitome of a self-on-the-throne mentality. It prohibits mature, loving relationships with the Lord and with others. Anything goes. Left to run wild, our selfish natures will take over like the kudzu weed in Florida.

Marriage provides a hothouse environment for selfishness to multiply, were it not for the Lord. As a husband and wife each leave self behind and move closer to Him, they automatically grow closer to one another. (Think of a triangle with "God" at the top point and "man" and "woman" at each of the other two points.)

That you may have pleasure in everything

Seek your own pleasure in nothing.

That you may know everything

Seek to know nothing.

That you may be everything

Seek to be nothing.

—Sᴛ. Jᴏʜɴ ᴏғ ᴛʜᴇ Cʀᴏss

Pistis, the Greek word for faith, must take root in a heart before the flower of genuine love can bloom. You don't believe me? First John 4:7 backs me up: "For love is from God, and everyone who loves is born of God and knows God" (NASB). Faith in Him means belief in who He is and what He says. By doubting the authenticity and authority of God's Word, we guarantee that the "survival-of-the-fittest" mentality will rule not only the animal kingdom, but also the human kingdom. We can then forget about the abundant joy that comes from commitment to His will.

Though an unbeliever's achievements sparkle by the world's standards, they cannot fool God, any more than a cubic zirconium can fool a diamond specialist. How quickly we forget! "Without faith it is impossible to please him: for he that cometh to God must believe that he is, and that he is a rewarder of them that diligently seek him" (Heb. 11:6).

ASSUMING THE WORST

Cynics, as Webster defines them, are "faultfinding, captious critics." Having lost the ability to appreciate the good in life, they focus on the negative almost to the exclusion of the positive. They wear a complaining attitude like a trademark. H. L. Mencken said, "A cynic is a man who, when he smells flowers, looks around for a coffin." Due to their pessimistic outlook, cynics find it difficult to submit to God and love others. In the 1950s, cardiologists Meyer Friedman and Ray Roseman discovered that impatient individuals, those who walked and ate in a rush, who interrupted others and complained constantly, were more likely to suffer heart problems. Friedman and Roseman labeled these caustic critics "Type A" personalities; their calmer counterparts they called "Type B." Follow-up studies conducted at various research

When a man sees that a neighbor hates him, then he must love him more than before to fill up the gap.

—Rabbi Rafael.

facilities supported these findings, and point to cynicism as a component of Type A behavior perhaps more damaging than others.

Duke University researcher Redford Williams administered a section of the Minnesota Multiphasic Personality Inventory (MMPI) that measures hostility and cynicism to more than fifteen hundred patients being examined for arteriosclerotic symptoms. Those with high levels of cynical, complaining behavior were fifty percent more likely to have clogged arteries than those who scored low. Since the MMPI has been used extensively since the 1950s, researchers consulted earlier test results and confirmed Williams's findings. One study of 255 physicians who took the test twenty-five years earlier showed that those with high "cynicism" scores had five times the level of heart disease as those who scored below the median.

At St. Luke's, we see a few patients who criticize *everything*. They feel upset with the world and do not appreciate any help they receive. Their selfishness damages not only them, but their families and friends as well.

On the other hand, many patients of St. Luke's send warm thank-you notes after they visit. How their kindness refreshes us! We work hard to demonstrate our motto, "Excellence With Love," and it's nice to know when we've succeeded. In their letters, people mention how much they enjoyed the natural beauty of the surroundings; and, always, they cite the staff—their soft voices, gentle touch and caring attitude. These anti-cynics appreciate life and the people around them, so their days become a joy rather than a drudgery.

Sometimes I wake up with a critical, cynical attitude, rather than a positive one of praise and adoration for the Lord. But I know I don't want to stay there. That's the key. The most important thing I can do in the early morning

So long as one loves, one forgives.

—FRANÇOIS DE LA ROCHEFOUCAULD

hours? Get rid of this poison. I fall short, and, invariably, it hinders my ability to love. My productivity at work also suffers. But when I walk close to the Lord and surrender my thoughts to Him, He nurtures a beautiful, mellow love between us that can flow to others around me during the day. A reminder in Philippians 4:8 keeps me on track:

> Finally, brethren, whatsoever things are true, whatsoever things are honest, whatsoever things are just, whatsoever things are pure, whatsoever things are lovely, whatsoever things are of good report; if there be any virtue, and if there be any praise, think on these things.

"YOU REALLY BUG ME"

I think it was Charlie Brown or Snoopy who made the profound statement, "I love humanity. It's people I can't stand." We can consider ourselves quite loving as long as we don't have to deal one-on-one with anybody. People rub us the wrong way at times, don't they? Funny thing. We do the same to them! We're just too self-centered to care.

No matter what our careers—whether as housewife, factory worker or doctor—dealing with people on a day-by-day basis can test our love quotient to the utmost. Those in the medical profession face special challenges, because patients only come to us with *problems*. Think about it. They rarely stop by when things are going well! (Of course, we wouldn't have time to see them if they did!) And if we doctors want to really sing the blues, we can go on about how exasperated we feel over government regulations, Medicare, the media, insurance, colleagues, lawyers...Little by little, frustration wears away our joy until we can no longer demonstrate a loving, peaceful spirit.

Some days when I'm especially irritable, I have to

Love must be learned, and learned

again and again; there is no end to

it. Hate needs no instruction but

wants only to be provoked.

—KATHERINE ANN PORTER

remind myself how fortunate I am to be able to practice medicine. I can love and care for others and get paid for it! I try to offer specific thanks to the Lord for each patient I see and for each operation I perform. Neglect the discipline of this practice, and I revert back to my selfish ways in a hurry. Only by maintaining a mental state of thankfulness and worship, have I even scratched the surface of real love. "In everything give thanks; for this is the will of God in Christ Jesus concerning you" (1 Thess. 5:18).

READY TO BLOW

With minimal provocation, your blood's boiling. Cheeks flush, breath quickens and muscles tense up. A verbal tirade chomps at the bit to storm the gate. We've all been in that situation numerous times, and regretted the aftermath. "A gentle answer turns away wrath, but a harsh word stirs up anger," Proverbs 15:1 reminds us (NASB). We choose to ignore those words of wisdom.

Anger and temper often result from a self-centered mind that wants its own way and doesn't get it. Foul emotions, if left unmanaged, will damage their owner and all his relationships.

Repressed anger can manifest itself as health problems—headaches, back pain, gastrointestinal disorders and severe depression, to name a few possibilities. Temporarily disabling, they prevent us from producing our best to glorify God. Even the sanctioned, semi-controlled tantrums people engage in during athletic events do untold harm.

I have had a problem with anger. Because of it, I have struggled to experience the joy of the Lord. My temper has improved gradually—not through personal effort, but as I spent time with the Lord and drew near to Him. I simply

It is natural to love those who love us, but it is supernatural to love those who hate us.

threw up the white flag and asked Him to help me. "He's still workin' on me," as the song goes; but the Holy Spirit has helped me control my anger to a great extent. He'll do the same for you. If we're full of the pure Holy Spirit, toxic waste will have no place to pile up.

One couple in our church, celebrating their fiftieth wedding anniversary, was asked, "What's your secret?"

They glanced at each other, smiled and both answered, "Forgiveness. We never went to bed mad." Good advice from some experts—and Ephesians 4:26. We'll look more at the power of forgiveness in the next section.

SOCIAL HOMICIDE

Hate destroys! Like a rusty splinter allowed to fester in a wound to the point of severe infection, hate intensifies from long-standing anger. Jesus went so far as to label this form of self-exaltation "murder"—a crime punishable by death in the Old Testament. Hate wounds deeply, both the one to whom it is directed, and the one who carries it around inside. Such extreme unforgiveness corrodes our spirits until we can't love anyone. Worse yet, it can make us capable of acts of untold violence. We've seen proof of this in the increase in workplace murders by disgruntled former employees.

Hate could have crippled me when I first started in private practice years ago. Let me share the story.

I was fortunate enough to know an optometrist who had been a high-ranking political official. He had a rare form of glaucoma. After I performed a successful operation, he sent letters of recommendation to the optometrists in the small town where I had relocated.

Now, in that same town, the ophthalmologists (M.D.s/surgeons of the eye) had been rather antagonistic

TEN STEPS TO CARNAL LIVING

1. Spend as much time watching secular television as you possibly can. You owe it to yourself!

2. Eat sweets often and give into every craving for food immediately.

3. Love yourself more, and God and others less.

4. Fill your life with fun things and avoid adversity at all cost.

5. Be a taker, not a giver; after all, you already pay taxes!

6. Never do anything that could be construed as fanaticism; you do have an image to uphold!

7. Don't worry about having daily devotions; you don't have time!

8. When you are confronted with sin in your life, go directly into delusion.

9. Anytime you have a problem, go straight to a psychology book; it knows much more about life than the Bible.

10. Give in to every sexual urge; after all, God created you with them.

—STEVE GALLAGHER
PURE LIFE MINISTRIES

to the optometrists. I treated them all with equal respect—
because it was the right thing to do. As a result, the
optometrists—a group of professionals who had always
been considered second-class citizens—sent many patients
my way who needed a specialist. Success was inevitable
with so many referrals. We used innovative techniques at
our clinic, which added fuel to the fire. *It should take years
to build a busy practice!* the others whispered among themselves. They gossiped, slandered, attacked and made life
very unpleasant. Some even resorted to outright sabotage.
I struggled hard against a build-up of hate inside me.
Fortunately, God's forgiveness won over my base nature.
For the most part, I maintained a peaceful attitude—with
the help of the Word and prayer.

In a hate-producing situation, simply doing for others is
also good therapy. Responding with a servant's heart to
those who have hurt us helps us release emotions and personal rights.

> Let all bitterness, and wrath, and anger, and clamour,
> and evil speaking, be put away from you, with all
> malice: and be ye kind one to another, tenderhearted,
> forgiving one another, even as God for Christ's sake
> hath forgiven you.
>
> —Ephesians 4:31–32

A college co-ed was raped on campus by a young man
and his friends. Understandably, for years, she hated them
for what they had done to her—until she accepted Jesus as
her Savior. Amazing! She forgave them at last and even told
them she loved them. God's powerful love, demonstrated
through this young lady, conquered unforgiveness and the
demonic powers of hell. "Hatred stirs up contentions, but
love covers all transgressions" (Prov. 10:12, AMP).

Could we forbear dispute and

practise love, we should agree as

angels do above.

—EDMUND WALLER

Forgiveness, one of the greatest characteristics of God, is so like Him and so unlike us. Without it, no man can experience the peace, love and joy of being a Christian. Jesus personified forgiveness. As He was dying on the cross, He prayed for those who crucified Him, "Father, forgive them; for they know not what they do" (Luke 23:34). He enables us to follow His example as we rest in His love. He transforms us into spiritual overcomers. We need to ask for forgiveness from God and others—over and over again. Hate and God, like oil and water, don't mix. "If a man say, I love God, and hateth his brother, he is a liar: for he that loveth not his brother whom he hath seen, how can he love God whom he hath not seen?" (1 John 4:20).

PART THREE

LOVE AT ITS FINEST

Our Goal Held High

The highest love of all finds its

fulfillment not in what it keeps,

but in what it gives.

—FR. ANDREWS, S.D.C.

Remember my conversation some thirty-one years ago with the kind, south-Georgia reverend? He surprised me with questions like "Why do you want to get married, Jim?" and "What do you mean by love?" I had the world by the tail...or so I thought. Marriage would be a piece of cake. And what newlywed doesn't believe that? (Just ask some of your friends to show you their wedding albums. See the euphoric expressions on their faces?)

Heather and I have learned so much since those early days. The good times, and yes, even the tough times, have taught us many things. Through it all, we've found genuine love to be rewarding...comforting...exhilarating...and sometimes excruciating *work* (that dirty four-letter word). Everything of value costs something to someone. Marriage is no exception. We get out of it what we put into it. Let me share a story to illustrate my point.

Imagine, for a moment, that you've been invited to a wedding. This one draws friends and family from near and far. The stunning bride, decked out in a fantastic gown, arrives at the sanctuary entrance on her father's arm. Her groom stands, quivering knees and all, at the altar. (He *should* quiver a little as he contemplates the magnitude of their decision.)

The beautiful ceremony goes according to plan: Scripture reading, music, pictures, candles, rings, *vows*... Vows. A limousine waits outside to drive them to the reception, and that, too, goes without a hitch. Food,

Love for God is ecstatic, making us

go out from ourselves; it does not

allow the lover to belong any more

to himself, but he belongs

only to the Beloved.

—ST. DIONYSIUS THE AREOPAGITE

music, guests, fun and more pictures. After the minimum amount of time required by etiquette, the newlyweds wave their good-byes and zip away to begin their new life as husband and wife...

But what if...rather than heading off to a honeymoon together, they were to embrace, climb into separate cars (each one decorated with "Just-Married" paraphernalia) and ride off in different directions?

What if, from this point on, the two continue as if the ceremony changed nothing? They live in separate houses and have separate agendas. As time permits, they may correspond once in a while, but if they don't get a chance to write as often as they should, at least they call every few months. Sometimes, that's the most they can manage. When someone questions their peculiar behavior, they admit, "Oh, we just wanted a wedding. We never intended to be husband and wife. Too much work. And besides, we're both so busy."

Ridiculous. People who marry intend to live together, to cherish each other and get to know one another better every day. They want to become one.

So they think.

We all *plan* to do just that, until the personal cost mounts after the honeymoon. We may never actually drive off to different destinations, other than for brief trips, but countless mates trudge through their days in mental, emotional and spiritual isolation. Of course, engaged couples think their marriage will be "the exception." Reality settles in soon after the fires of infatuation dwindle a bit.

Marital bliss doesn't happen overnight. It requires time and patience, but most of all, it requires a major change in attitude—a change from a preoccupation with self to a passion for the other person. Dare we do anything less than

To love and be loved

the wise would give

All that for which alone

the unwise live.

—WALTER SAVAGE LANDOR

show God's grace to the one we vow to love until death?

God saves us by grace. We can't take an ounce of credit. (See Romans 3:24; 5:15; Ephesians 2:5.) He cares about us as much as He does His own perfect Son. His love burns as strong for us now as it will in heaven when He transforms us from head to toe. We need only appropriate that truth into our hearts. That should leave us standing in awe. What magnificent, unmerited goodness He shows us!

In case we have questions about how far we should go, in turn, for a beloved, God sets the standard for us. He sent Jesus. He gave Himself unto death for a reason—to wipe the slate clean between us and the Father.

The apostle John leaves no room for doubt about ultimate love. (See John 3:16 and 1 John 3:16.) It requires ultimate sacrifice; a readiness to lay down our most prized possession—our lives—for someone else. And not just someone who loves us back, either. An enemy! Outrageous. A commitment to God's will demands a willingness to go that far.

We cannot comprehend a love so intense. Would I offer my children to serve time in prison in someone else's place? Would you? God did just that for us! The greatest human love shrinks to nothing by comparison.

We can never add to what Jesus accomplished on the cross, but what if God does call on us to suffer or even die, so that another can know Him? Have we considered that possibility? Are we ready? Martyrdom may never enter the picture for most of us. However, He does call us to love our family members at their grouchiest and whiniest moments. Essentially, we lay down our lives by giving up our "rights" to our own way and our personal comfort.

Peter, the apostle, overrated his devotion to Jesus. When the pressure intensified on the night before Jesus' death, and

Love may be a fool's paradise, but it

is the only paradise we know

on this troubled planet.

—ROBERT BLATCHFORD

it threatened his own neck, Peter flunked the love test with flying colors. He denied three times, *once with curses*, that he knew Jesus at all. We'd best not look down our noses at the poor guy, though. How like him we are! Especially as we stand before the altar of the living God, radiant in our wedding finery, and make brash promises to love forever, under all conditions, an imperfect human being.

We, like Peter, vastly overestimate ourselves. And so, like Peter, we end up flat on our faces, weeping, in the muck of failure. Enter, hope. Jesus of Nazareth! After His resurrection, Jesus reassured Peter in a very personal way that He held no grudges. He "reinstated" him in front of his peers.

He also asked Peter a pointed question, "Do you love me more than these?" using the word for self-sacrificing love—*agape*. Peter answered using *phileo*, as in "Yes, Lord, I love you as a friend." Jesus responded with an *agape* kind of directive, "Feed My lambs." In other words, "It doesn't matter so much how you say it, Peter. Show Me your love by caring for those I love."

Why did Jesus ask Peter three times if he loved Him? He knew without asking. I don't know for sure. Perhaps, He was giving Peter a chance to admit the truth: his helplessness to show *agape* love in his own strength.

Only when we fully experience God's love, can we accomplish one of the most difficult tasks we will ever be called to do—to love the unlovable. Jesus did when He walked the earth, and He does now. He loves prostitutes, lepers, the demon-possessed and even murderers. With his *agape* love filling us, we will find it more natural to love those who may not be very pleasant.

This kind of love reigns as the undisputed sign of a committed Christian. In chapter thirteen of his first letter to the Corinthian church, Paul paints a clear picture of *agape*.

What must come first in all prayers,

however varied they may be, and

what gives them real value is the

love with which they are made.

—CHARLES DE FOUCAULD

As a powerful deterrent and stimulant, it hedges our way from wrongdoing and opens the door to righteousness.

Colossians 3:14 admonishes, "And above all things, put on charity, which is the bond of perfectness." The King James translation of *love* in these passages, "charity," loses impact on modern readers. Charity, to us, consists of an occasional donation to non-profit organizations. That does not scratch the surface of what true *agape* involves: a complete heart attitude and way of life.

First Corinthians 13 mentions nine characteristics of love:

> Patience: Love suffers long…
> Kindness: And is kind…
> Generosity: Love envies not…
> Humility: Love vaunts not itself, is not puffed up…
> Courtesy: Does not behave itself unseemly…
> Unselfishness: Seeks not her own…
> Good Temper: Is not easily provoked…
> Guilelessness: Thinks no evil…
> Sincerity: Rejoices not in iniquity, but rejoices in the truth…

Jesus' beloved disciple, John, described love beautifully in 1 John 4:7–21. I offer it as our goal in life. The following passage from the Amplified Bible is rather long, I know, but before you scrunch up your face, just try reading and meditating on it. Take it in bite-sized pieces, if you must. The Amplified version gives additional shades of meaning from the original Greek text:

> *Beloved, let us love one another; for love is (springs) from God; and he who loves [his fellowmen] is begotten (born) of God and is coming [progressively] to know and understand God [to perceive and recognize and get a better and clearer knowledge of Him]. He who does not love*

To love as Jesus loves; that is not

only the Lord's precept, it is our

vocation. When all is said and done,

it is the only thing we have to learn,

for it is perfection.

—RENÉ VOILLAUME

has not become acquainted with God [does not and never did know Him], for God is love. In this the love of God was made manifest (displayed) where we are concerned: in that God sent His Son, the only begotten or unique [Son], into the world so that we might live through Him. In this is love: not that we loved God, but that He loved us and sent His Son to be the propitiation (the atoning sacrifice) for our sins. Beloved, if God loved us so [very much], we also ought to love one another. No man has at any time [yet] seen God. But if we love one another, God abides (lives and remains) in us and his love (that love which is essentially His) is brought to completion (to its full maturity, runs its full course, is perfected) in us! By this we come to know (perceive, recognize, and understand) that we abide (live and remain) in Him and He in us: because He has given (imparted) to us of His [Holy] Spirit. And [besides] we ourselves have seen (have deliberately and steadfastly contemplated) and bear witness that the Father has sent the Son [as the] Savior of the world. Anyone who confesses (acknowledges, owns) that Jesus is the Son of God, God abides (lives, makes His home) in him and he [abides, lives, makes his home] in God. And we know (understand, recognize, are conscious of, by observation and experience) and believe (adhere to and put faith in and rely on) the love God cherishes for us. God is love, and he who dwells and continues in love dwells and continues in God, and God dwells and continues in him. In this [union and communion with Him] love is brought to completion and attains perfection with us, that we may have confidence for the day of judgment [with assurance and boldness to face Him] because as He is, so are we in this world. There is no fear in love [dread does not exist], but full-grown (complete, perfect) love turns fear out of doors and expels every trace of terror! For fear

Christian love represents both being and doing. Change on the inside affects what we do on the outside.

*brings with it the thought of punishment, and [so] he
who is afraid has not reached the full maturity of love [is
not yet grown into love's complete perfection]. We love
Him, because He first loved us. If anyone says, I love
God, and hates (detests, abominates) his brother [in
Christ], he is a liar; for he who does not love his brother,
whom he has seen, cannot love God, Whom he has not
seen. And this command (charge, order, injunction) we
have from Him: that he who loves God shall love his
brother [believer] also.*

"How can I love like that?" you may ask. "I never could
and never will."

Three cheers. The light of truth has dawned. Neither
can I, so join the club. Let's just be honest enough to admit
it and go on from here.

So then, how *do* imperfect, sinful, selfish folks like us
ever love as God insists that we love? We have touched on
the subject, and we'll talk more about it in depth. First,
though, let me tell you an ancient legend.

One day, a wicked, ugly old man saw a beautiful young
woman who captured his heart. Wanting to court her, he put
on a Prince Charming mask. He portrayed the part so well
that he won the maiden's hand. Five years after their marriage, a longtime enemy showed up on the scene who sought
to destroy the image he had assumed. He snatched off the old
man's disguise. To everyone's amazement, the face beneath
the handsome mask was no longer that of a wretched old
man. He had actually turned into Prince Charming!

In the spiritual world, masks don't work, of course.
Religion has tried to get us to wear them for centuries, to
no avail. No way to zap us from wretches into princes,
fairy-tale style. We need that real gut-level transformation,
from the inside out.

To love at all is to be vulnerable. Love anything and your heart will certainly be wrung and possibly be broken. If you want to make sure of keeping it intact, you must give your heart to no one, not even to an animal. Wrap it carefully round with hobbies and little luxuries; avoid all entanglements; bolt it up safe in the casket or coffin of your selfishness. But in that casket—safe, dark, motionless, airless—it will change. It will not be broken; it will become unbreakable, impenetrable, irredeemable... The only place outside Heaven where you can be perfectly safe from all the dangers of love... is Hell.

—C. S. Lewis

However, we do become what we *commit* to and *focus on* all the time. If we focus on Jesus, He "conforms us to His likeness," which is love. If we focus on evil, we resemble it before long. The apostle Paul writes in 2 Corinthians 3:18, "But we all, with open face beholding as in a glass the glory of the Lord, are changed into the same image from glory to glory, even as by the Spirit of the Lord."

Marriage provides the consummate opportunity to tear off the masks and bring about an inner change from ugly to beautiful, from selfishness to the highest kind of love— *commitment.* A committed person will exhibit *agape* love. Commitment has a way of bringing us under the Lord's direction as nothing else can.

Now that I think about it, even a godly quality like this can turn into self-servitude. For example, people enter into a legal marriage, sanctioned by society, and behave according to expected cultural and religious beliefs. They say they love each other. In truth, after a short time, duty alone binds them together. They tolerate each other and cohabit…but love? No. The normal problems of life upset their fragile union and prove their lack of love. This counterfeit of true commitment rings false. It leads to a cold, dead marriage.

Why would mates refuse to appreciate each others' thoughts, passions, feelings and dreams, yet vow through clenched teeth to hold the marriage together, no matter what? Why resign themselves to such a dismal fate? For any number of selfish reasons. Appearances. Convenience. Financial security. Fear of being alone.

No *human* ability can fulfill the marriage vow to love a spouse forever. Given bad breath, indigestion and who knows how many other unpleasant occurrences of normal living, it's impossible for anyone to love another forever.

Over the long haul, only those things of the Spirit will last.

Love in your heart wasn't put there

to stay. Love isn't love 'til

you give it away.

The wife who stands by her husband, without reservation, when he loses his job, sets an example of commitment. The husband who remains faithful to his wife when she falls prey to a chronic illness, does also. These marriages have formed a bond not easily destroyed because Jesus Christ is the divine super glue in the middle. The author of Ecclesiastes knew the power of a God-centered marriage, as we see from his words: "And if one prevail against him, two shall withstand him; and a threefold cord is not quickly broken" (Eccles. 4:12).

All good marriages possess a common, solid-gold core of commitment. A fifty-year-old professional I know fell in love with a beautiful middle-aged lady. He faced a major challenge—she suffered a partial handicap from multiple sclerosis. He married her, knowing full well that he would spend his life waiting on her. In time, she did become bedridden, but he continued to express selfless devotion toward her.

Even more amazing, a newspaper featured a story of a young couple who experienced an unbelievable crisis. On the first day of their island honeymoon, the new bride frolicked in the water. She was standing in a slight hole, so the water appeared deeper than it was.

Her husband plunged headlong into the water to join her. Snap! He broke his neck. In only seconds, their lives changed forever. Can you comprehend their devastation? Young, healthy, with dreams of the future, now facing quadriplegia. Many young women would have left, pronto. Not this young wife. She remained faithful to her husband. Today, they await the birth of a baby through artificial insemination, and they enjoy the deepest love possible.

A poem from my book, *The Dynamics of Worship*, describes commitment better than I can:

A dear old Quaker lady who was

asked what gave her such a lovely

complexion and what cosmetic she

used, replied sweetly: "I use for the

lips, truth; for the voice, prayer; for

the eyes, pity; for the hands, charity;

for the figure, uprightness;

and for the heart, love."

Commitment is what transforms a promise into reality.
It is the words that speak boldly of your intentions
And the actions which speak louder than words.
It is making the time...when there is none.
Coming through time after time, year after year.
Commitment is the stuff character is made of;
The power to change the face of things.
It is the daily triumph of integrity over skepticism.

—AUTHOR UNKNOWN

Who was the greatest lover in the Bible, other than Jesus? Was it David? Solomon? Hosea, perhaps? Hosea wins my vote. That man showed undying commitment to his wife, Gomer, despite her blatant unfaithfulness to him. In many ways, we, like Gomer and Hosea, are tapestries of selfishness and selflessness. To the degree we imitate Hosea, we become true Christian lovers.

Ultimate commitment means ultimate love.

The level of forgiveness Hosea showed does not come easily, especially when it concerns a painful issue like an adulterous spouse. God put this story in His Word for a reason. It reminds us how much He loves and forgives us, and at the same time sets the example. We have no right to expect perfection in our spouses. To do so only leads to misery.

As I see it, such commitment forms the backbone of Christian love. In fact, we could say that *commitment* is to *love* what the *skeleton* is to the human *body*. Although its somewhat ungainly appearance doesn't arouse many amorous feelings, where would a body be without the skeleton's strength and substance?

Such pure love exists only in God. We cannot conjure it up or duplicate it. Something wonderful happens when our spirit surrenders to His. An unfathomable love overflows to

While some books inform and others reform, only the Bible transforms.

us. It activates commitment between any two of God's children who share a mutual faith in the Father's promises. God pours Himself into our hearts through the Holy Spirit (Romans 5:5), until our love for others conforms to His love for us.

In fact, dual forces act in concert to bring about this change in us from natural to supernatural love. The Holy Spirit acts through us to the degree that we allow Him free reign (James 4:5). At the same time, the decision rests with us whether or not to abide by such a commitment.

This union of God's Spirit and the human spirit produces positive results in our lives. Neither works independently of the other, but rather they work "in partnership." We could think of a safe deposit box—two keys open it. The customer uses one key and the bank's agent uses the other at the same time. God ordained our relationship with Him to work in a similar way. (Not that He *had* to, mind you.)

The Holy Spirit is too much of a gentleman to force Himself on us, and our meager human resources cannot produce good, lasting fruit without Him. In time, He begins forming His loving nature in us. Just as selfishness manifests itself in many ways, so does love, through the fruit of the Spirit: (love), joy, peace, longsuffering, gentleness, goodness, faith, meekness and temperance (Galatians 5:22). (Notice how this fruit resembles the characteristics of love from 1 Corinthians 13.)

As a young Christian, and still very much a carnal man, the committed life lay far beyond my grasp. Only with God's fulfilling presence in me could I accept His love, accept myself, love Him in turn and be a vessel from which His love flowed to others.

If I didn't know the Source of love very well, how could I express it? I couldn't! I had to totally identify with Him to

Any man who is too busy to pray is

busier than God intended

him to be.

escape the destruction of my own selfish mind. As long as I was in control, I couldn't do away with me, if you know what I mean. The Holy Spirit had to direct my love and empower my commitment before I experienced God's kind of love.

Even after all these years of walking with the Lord, I still like to think I can accomplish a whole lot more on my own than I actually can. I struggle to commit and submit myself wholeheartedly to Him, and so I struggle to love. Oh, the passionate longing to do so may be there, and I may very well accomplish a few things in my own strength, but the rewards don't last.

On the other hand, when God's love flows into my heart, it spreads peace and fulfillment within me. I feel good about my Christian walk. I feel good about life. I feel good about others. Mere human passion can never do this. It teases and pleases for a while, then leaves us empty, craving more.

To become a reliable vessel through which God's love flows unrestrained, I have had to first accept that love fully myself. I can only pass on what I have experienced.

Here's an example of that principle. In Central Florida we have people born and raised in a southern climate, many of whom have never seen a single snowflake. They have never numbed their ungloved fingers on a snowball, or felt the elation of skiing down a snow-covered hill in the crisp morning air. How well could they understand such experiences? How accurate could their instructions be about what to do in that kind of circumstance? Likewise, with love; we must savor the taste of divine grace before we can demonstrate it to anyone else. Not only once at salvation, but *every day*.

Remember that beautiful passage about love from the fourth chapter of First John? Verses seven and eight say, "Love is from God; and everyone who loves is born of God and knows God" (NASB). That means if we would love as

We only deliberately waste time with those we love—it is the purest sign that we love someone if we choose to spend time idly in their presence when we could be doing something more constructive.

—SHEILA CASSIDY

God intends for us to love, we must get to know Him intimately. He supplies the method and the means. We remain
very much His passive instruments—plain old empty vessels holding His love and His Word mixed with prayer.

Just as friendships between people vary in their degree of
intimacy, so do relationships with God. Most everyone
claims to want closeness with Him, but few persevere in
prayer and the Word until they feel His presence. Most
quit far short of what they say they would like.

A hyperactive "self-life" stands somewhere between us
and the fulfillment of that desire. To develop intimacy—
on any level but especially with God—we must do away
with our preoccupation with and protection of self. No
other option. Peter showed us the cure—drop our guard,
as well as our brotherly (*phileo*) love, where God is concerned. Let the Holy Spirit fill us with *agape* from the top
of our heads to the soles of our feet. Then, not only the
things we say, but the lives we live, will bring glory to Him.

Ultimately, life presents us with countless choices every
day. Most are so insignificant, we may not even realize we've
made conscious decisions, but we have. The process starts in
the morning before we get out of bed. We all decide which
way we will love, which way we will live and which way we
will act. One of life's blessings lies in our right to choose
between good and evil, between positive and negative mental attitudes. A choice to love depends entirely on our level
of commitment. If we want love, we really have only one
choice: to love Jesus Christ with all our hearts, souls and
minds. That's the million-dollar variable. Will we set aside
enough time to become super-close companions of the
omnipotent living God, or will we settle for a pretentious
interview with Him whenever we get in a pinch?

There's no secret formula for intimacy with the Lord.

The more thou thine own self

Out of thy self dost throw

The more will into thee

God with his Godhead flow.

—ANGELUS SILESIUS

We nurture it by reading and meditating on the Word and spending time in prayer. He wants ample time to "speak" to our hearts. During those precious moments when we're quiet before Him, the loving Master enfolds us in His tender embrace. He refreshes and renews.

Let's be honest: God cares less about the words we say, the titles we wear or the works we do, than He does about our desire for intimacy with Him. Why? He knows if *He* takes first place, the rest will fall in line. That's why Jesus urged His followers, "Abide in Me and I in you" (John 15:4).

The Lord wants us just to sit still with Him awhile, to "stay put" and enjoy being in His presence. "Abiding in Him" implies a depth of closeness far beyond the "hip-pocket prayers" uttered on the run sometime between the moment our feet hit the floor and the time we dash madly out the door for work.

As children of God, we derive our strength from this abiding. Said another way, we need intense commitment to Him. We can acknowledge God, prefer God, have faith in God, worship God, have fellowship with Him and study His Word...but unless we dedicate ourselves to Him, we fall far short of our Christian calling of holiness.

Love, like a collage or tapestry, blends many disjointed aspects of life into a whole. The five basic kinds of love we mentioned at the beginning of the book (*epithumia*, *eros*, *philia*, *storge* and *agape*), overlap and shift along the entire spectrum from selfishness to commitment. In other words love ranges from one hundred percent *taking* all the way to one hundred percent *giving*. God maintains perfect balance.

A golden thread of commitment winds its way through the tapestry of human relationships, strengthening and beautifying them for God's glory. It touches friends and

To the Christian, death is not an end, but an event in life; a new start with an extended knowledge, and a purer love.

—BISHOP OF LINCOLN

family, and fills moments of marital intimacy with divine satisfaction.

The opposite is also true, as much as I wish it weren't. Selfishness sneaks into everything good and spoils the design from above. Not even the most noble loves are safe from its influence. At any time, the relationship between two people can cross a fine line where selfish emotions spoil good intentions. If we're wise, we'll guard against such traps.

Think about the compassionate Christian employer whose secretary is going through a divorce. She's hurting. He cares about her, and doesn't want her to suffer in silence, so he lends a listening ear. He means well. Before long though, his platonic compassion takes an unexpected turn—to passion. Neither of them recognizes the danger signals until it's too late. They become sexually intimate— and now two families go to divorce court instead of one.

The cross of Calvary, however, is a positive example of the shifting of virtue, from bad to good. Crucifying Jesus stands alone as the world's worst sin. Thank God, it did not end that way. God turned it around and made it the most monumental event in history.

Let's review several main points about love we have covered throughout the book: 1) We cannot love because we're too selfish. 2) Only God can truly love. He is love. 3) God's *agape* love must flow to and through us by His Holy Spirit. 4) For that to happen, we must get close to Him. 5) His Word and prayer become mandatory lifelines.

And the catalyst for all these interactions? *Commitment. Commitment. Commitment!* Dr. Stephen Olford defines that favorite word of mine this way: "faithful, fervent and focused." Amen!

Love is the energy of life, with all it

yields of joy or woe and hope and

fear, is just our chance o' the prize of

learning love—How love might be,

hath been indeed, and is.

—BROWNING

Epilogue

All of life is an endless cycle. We see signs throughout the universe: The sun rises and sets. The moon waxes and wanes, causing the tides to rise and fall on every ocean beach in the world. The stars, and their myriad constellations, are in a continual state of flux. Seasons come and go. Not even the huge glaciers of the frozen north remain static. Our lives move in cycles. We're born, grow up, mature, grow old and die.

What kind of world would we have if newborn babies never developed physically beyond those first few moments outside the womb? Hard to imagine. A generation or so later, there wouldn't be anyone to reproduce or care for others. It doesn't take a genius to see that this old earth wouldn't last long under those conditions. Yet, spiritually, a great number of us do just that. We never grow up.

Ideally, change should continue over the course of a believer's lifetime. The born-again experience *should* mark the birth of the ultimate loving relationship with the Lord. I have found that relationship to be dynamic and exciting, a union that endures and grows. Commitment to God's will has challenged me to the utmost. It demands every ounce of discipline from me. Being an avid participant in endurance sports, I can state without reservation that commitment to God's will is even more challenging, but it makes me a better spouse, lover, father, athlete and doctor.

When we reach our golden years, "the autumn of life," most of us realize that those things which once seemed so important, really aren't at all. We attain a measure of wisdom.

Love makes obedience a thing of joy!
To do the will of one we like to please
Is never hardship, though it tax our strength;
Each privilege of service love will seize!
Love makes us loyal, glad to do our go,
And eager to defend a name or cause;
Love takes the drudgery from common work,
And asks no rich reward or great applause.
Love gives us satisfaction in our task,
And wealth in learning lessons of the heart;
Love sheds a light of glory on our toil
And makes us humbly glad to have a part.
Love makes us choose to do the will of God,
to run His errands and proclaim His truth;
It gives our hearts an eager, lilting song;
Our feet shod with tireless wings of youth!

—HAZEL HARTWELL SIMON

Of course, not everyone learns this invaluable lesson, but in the end, it doesn't matter. We have no choice but to relinquish our hold and release all we've received—youth, health, wealth, loved ones. Whether we do it willingly, or fight against the inevitable with all our might, the things of this world fade away. But we can choose the manner in which we surrender by shifting our focus from the temporal to the external. To God Himself, the essence of love.

You know, this whole vast topic of love breaks down into three simple steps found in First John. Billy Graham's daughter, the fantastic Bible teacher Anne Graham Lotz, states them this way: 1) God's love for us; 2) Our love for God; 3) Our love for others. We need all three. *In that order.* Personalize those phrases now. Try saying to yourself, "God loves me. If I love God, I *can* love others."

In closing, I am reminded of the clever battery commercial starring two cartoon rabbit figures. They march along, with batteries on their backs, beating their little bass drums. The first rabbit falls flat on his face early in the commercial. (Of course, he isn't equipped with the right brand.) "Bunny #2" sports the right battery, so he keeps on marching and marching and marching and marching...

That's us, plugged into "God's battery." We keep on loving and serving and loving and serving...

Why not make a commitment to the real thing?

Natural love wears out; supernatural love endures.

Start today. Just *LOVE.*

Appendix

The Beatitudes of Love

Blessed are those who find love everywhere, for they may never be lonely.

Blessed are those who always give love, for they shall always have more love to give.

Blessed are those who make it easier for others to love them, for they shall always have plenty of friends.

Blessed are those who always communicate in love, for they are channels of blessing wherever they go.

Blessed are those who bestow healing love, for they may be known as the physicians of the soul.

Blessed are those who leave love wherever they go, for the world will be a better place because they have lived.

Blessed are those who love to work, for theirs is the kingdom of service.

Blessed are those who love to share, for theirs is the kingdom of joy everywhere.

Blessed are those who love to wait, for theirs is the kingdom of patience.

Blessed are those who love to praise others, for theirs is the kingdom of appreciation.

Blessed are those who love to put others first, for theirs is the kingdom of humility.

Blessed are those who love to be courteous, for theirs is the kingdom of good manners.

Blessed are those who love God first, and above all, for theirs is the kingdom of right relationship to God, people and things.

Blessed are those who love Jesus Christ, for they share His tender compassion for the whole world.

Blessed are those who love and receive the Holy Spirit, for theirs is the kingdom of holiness.

Blessed are those who love what is right and good, for theirs is the kingdom of justice and mercy.

Blessed are those who practice love in relation to all people at all times, for theirs is the kingdom of intimate kindness.

Blessed are those who plan to practice love always, for they shall live in the house of love and dwell in the city of God forever and ever.

—FROM *FORTY DAYS OF LOVE*
BY THOMAS A. CARRUTH

How Important Is Love to God?

Eagerly pursue and seek to acquire [this] love.

—1 Corinthians 14:1, AMP

Whereas the object and *purpose of our instruction* and *charge is love.*

—1 Timothy 1:5, AMP

Pursue righteousness, faith, love.

—2 Timothy 2:22, NASB

Let the love of the brethren continue.

—Hebrews 13:1, NASB

Love covers a multitude of sins.

—1 Peter 4:8, NASB

Love is from God.

—1 John 4:7, NASB

Keep yourselves in the love of God.

—Jude 21, NASB

He will quiet you in His love.

—Zephaniah 3:17, NIV

And above all these [put on] love…

—Colossians 3:14, AMP

He who has My commandments and keeps them, he it is who loves Me; and he who loves Me shall be loved by My Father, and I will love him, and will disclose Myself to him.

—John 14:21, NASB

WHAT DID JESUS DO AND ASK US TO DO IN LOVE?

I give you a new commandment—love one another as I have loved you (see John 13:34).

Love your enemies, show kindness to those who hate you, bless those who curse you. Pray for those who insult you (see Luke 6:27–28).

If you love Me you will take my commands to heart (see John 14:15).

The Golden Rule of Love—Do to others whatever you would wish them to do to you (see Matthew 7:12).

Whenever you stand up to pray, forgive any grievance that you have against anyone; that your Father who is in Heaven also may forgive you your offenses (see Mark 11:25).

Then Jesus took some bread, and after saying the thanksgiving, broke it and gave it to them, with these words: "This is My body which is now to be given on your behalf. Do this in memory of Me" (see Luke 22:19).

Father, forgive them; they do not know what they are doing (see Luke 23:34).

Be ready to make friends with your opponent (see Matthew 5:25).

If anyone strikes you on the right cheek, turn the other to him also (see Matthew 5:39).

If your brother does wrong, go to him and convince him of his fault when you and he are alone (see Matthew 18:15).

MORE PROVERBS OF LOVE

The happiest mind is the mind that cares for others.

We see God's love within us as we gaze inward; we know what we are and what God makes us. This change is proof of the reality and beauty of God's love.

When we walk deep in the Word, we have deep faith and love. When we walk shallow in the Word, we have shallow faith and love.

Our prayers should conform to the Word of God. A true love prayer to God springs out of His Word which is written on the tables of our hearts.

When we are free from inhibitions to express our love to God through worship and praise, the Holy Spirit releases us to love others.

Where love is, God is. He that dwells in love dwells in God. God is Love. Therefore, love—love—love: the poor, where it is easy; the rich, who need it most; our equals, where it is difficult; without distinction, without calculation, without procrastination.

We love because He first loved us. Love begets love.

Eloquence without love is noise. Love is greater than faith as the end is greater than the means. Love is greater than charity as the whole is greater than the parts.

Commitment to the Lordship of Christ brings continual revival and joy in the heart.

Your money is only as good as what you do with it.

—JOHN D. ROCKEFELLER

In matters of love, the beginning of the end often turns out to be but the end of the beginning.

Self-discipline never means giving up everything, for giving up is a loss. Our Lord did not ask us to give up the things of the earth, but to exchange them for better things.

—FULTON J. SHEEN

Love, like a spring rain, is pretty hard to be in the middle of without getting some on you.

—THE COUNTRY PARSON

A lovelorn porcupine was taking an evening stroll when he bumped into a cactus. "Is that you, sweetheart?" he asked tenderly.

Respect is what we owe; love, what we give.

—BAILEY

Love is a fruit in season at all times, and within the reach of every hand.

—MOTHER TERESA OF CALCUTTA

All for love, and nothing for reward.

—EDMUND SPENSER

To love is to admire with the heart: to admire is to love with the mind.

—T. GAUTIER

Money will buy a fine dog, but only love will make him wag his tail.

A successful marriage is one in which you fall in love many times, always with the same person.

—MCLAUGLIN

Don't marry someone you can live with. Marry someone you can't live without.

—JOSH MCDOWELL

A fine wedding and the marriage license do not make the marriage; it is the union of two hearts that welds husband and wife together.

Love is the only weapon we need.

—REV. H. R. L. SHEPPARD

The three great essentials of happiness are:
  Something to do,
  Someone to love
  And something to hope for.

We flatter those we scarcely know,
and please our fleeting guest;
But render many a heartless blow
to those we love the best.

Love is never afraid of giving too much.

Love is the fulfillment of the law.

—Paul, Romans 13:10

There is a Love always over you which you may reject but cannot alienate; there is a Friend always with you who, even in your loneliest moments, leaves you not alone...that Love, that Friend, is God in Christ.

—Ames Decker Holcomb

LOVE—the Greatest!

THE WEDDING COVENANT

How does a covenant differ from a contract?
A covenant is based on trust between parties.
A contract is based on distrust.
A covenant is based on unlimited responsibility.
A contract is based on limited liability.
A covenant cannot be broken if new circumstances occur.
A contract can be voided by mutual consent.

What is the significance of a white runner in the aisle?
It is a symbol of walking on holy ground. A covenant is not made merely between two people and their witnesses. It is made in the presence of God, and He is actively involved in the agreement, since it is God who joins them together. (See Matthew 19:6.)

Why does the groom enter the sanctuary before the bride and make the vows first?
The groom signifies that he is the covenant initiator. This is important because whoever initiates the covenant assumes greater responsibility for seeing it fulfilled. God initiated covenants with Noah, Abraham and David. Christ initiated the covenant of salvation with us. God is still at work to fulfill His covenants, and Christ will soon appear with the sound of trumpets to consummate the wedding with His bride, the Church. (See 1 Thessalonians 4:14–17.)

Why does the minister ask the question, "Who gives this woman to be married to this man?"

This question and its response symbolize not only the full blessing of the parents, but also the transfer of responsibility to the groom by the father. A daughter is under the authority and responsibility of her father until she is married. (See Numbers 30:4–8.)

Why do the bride and groom take each other's right hand during the wedding vows?

The open right hand offered by each party symbolizes their strength, resources and purpose. By clasping each other's right hands, they are pledging these to each other. Just as we depend upon the "saving strength of God's right hand," so each partner can depend upon all the resources that the other brings to the covenant relationship. (See Psalm 20:6.)

What is the real significance of the wedding rings?

In Scripture, the ring is a symbol of authority and the resources which go with it. (See Esther 8:2.) Also, whenever two parties made a covenant, they exchanged something of value as a token of their pledge. (See 1 Samuel 18:1–4.)

What is the purpose of introducing the new couple?

The introduction of the new couple establishes their change of names. In the marriage, the wife takes on the name of the husband, and the man becomes known as the husband of the wife. This name change is clearly illustrated in the covenant between Jehovah God and Abram. (See Genesis 17:4–5.)

Why does the couple sign wedding papers?

The couple signs wedding papers—a public document—
to establish a public record of the covenant. God wrote out
the testimony of His covenant in Scripture.

What is the significance of signing the guest book?

The guests become the official witnesses to the covenant.
By signing their names they are saying, "I have witnessed
the vows, and I will testify to the reality of this marriage."
The witnesses can also serve as God's reminders to the couple to be faithful to their marriage vows.

Why is a special invitation given for the wedding?

The invitation for the wedding symbolizes the invitation
to salvation. In the teaching ministry of Christ, He used
the invitation to the wedding feast as an illustration of
inviting people to partake of salvation. The wedding feast
was free to the invited guests, just as salvation is free to all
who will receive it. (See Isaiah 55:1.)

Why does the couple feed cake to each other?

This act symbolizes their becoming one flesh. By feeding
cake to each other, they are saying, "This represents my
body. As you eat it, I am becoming a part of you; and as I
eat the cake that you give to me, you become a part of me."
A New Testament illustration of this type of symbolism is
in the Lord's Supper. Jesus took bread, broke it and gave it
to His disciples saying, "Take, eat; this is my body, which
is broken for you...After the same manner also he took
the cup..." (See Matthew 26:26–27; 1 Corinthians
11:24–25.)

Bibliography

Bartlett, John, comp. *Familiar Quotations,* 10th ed., rev. and enl. by Haskell Dole. Boston: Little, Brown and Company, 1980.

Braude, Jacob M. *Speaker's Desk Book of Quips, Quotes and Anecdotes.* Saddle River, NJ: Prentice-Hall, Inc., 1963.

Dake's Annotated Reference Bible. Lawrenceville, GA: Dake Bible Sales, Inc.,1995

Edwards, Jonathan. *Charity and Its Fruits.* Carlisle, PA: The Banner of Truth Trust, 1991.

Edwards, Judson. *What They Never Told Us About How to Get Along With Each Other.* Eugene, OR: Harvest House Publishers, Inc., 1991.

Friedman, M. and R. H. Roseman. *Type A Behavior and Your Heart.* New York: Knopf, 1974.

Hyden, O. Quentin. *A Christian's Handbook of Psychiatry.* New York: Fleming H. Revel Co., 1976.

McLellan, Vern. *Love Lines.* Eugene, OR: Harvest House Publishers, Inc., 1990.

Pepper, Margaret. *The Harper Religious and Inspirational Quotation Companion.* New York: Harper & Row Publishers, Inc., 1989.

Piaget, Jean. *Psychology of the Child.* New York: Basic Books, 1969.

Tan, Paul Lee. *Encyclopedia of 7,700 Illustrations.* Dallas: Bible Communications, Inc., 1991.

ABOUT THE AUTHOR

James P. Gills, M.D., is founder and director of St. Luke's Cataract and Laser Institute in Tarpon Springs, Florida. Internationally respected as a cataract surgeon, Dr. Gills has performed more cataract extractions with lens implantations than anyone else in the world. He has pioneered many advancements in the field of ophthalmology to make cataract surgery safer and easier.

As a world-renowned ophthalmologist, Dr. Gills has received innumerable medical and educational awards, highlighted by 1994–2004 listings in *The Best Doctors in America*. Dr. Gills is a clinical professor of ophthalmology at The University of South Florida, and was named one of the Best Ophthalmologists in America in 1996 by ophthalmic academic leaders nationwide. He has served on the Board of Directors of the American College of Eye Surgeons, the Board of Visitors at Duke University Medical Center, and the Advisory Board of Wilmer Ophthalmological Institute at Johns Hopkins University. He has published more than 185 medical papers and authored nine medical textbooks. Listed in Marquis' *Who's Who in America*, Dr. Gills was Entrepreneur of the Year 1990 for the State of Florida, received the Tampa Bay Business Hall of Fame Award in 1993 and the Tampa Bay Ethics Award from the University of Tampa in 1995. In 1996 he was awarded the prestigious Innovators Award by his colleagues in the American Society of Cataract and Refractive Surgeons. In 2000 he was presented with the Florida Enterprise Medal by the Merchants Association of Florida, named Humanitarian of the Year by the Golda Meir/Kent Jewish Center in Clearwater, and Free Enterpriser of the Year by the Florida Council on Economic Education. In 2001 The Salvation Army presented Dr. Gills their prestigious "Others" Award in honor of his lifelong commitment to service and caring.

Virginia Polytechnic Institute, Dr. Gills' alma mater, presented their University Distinguished Achievement Award to him in

2003. In that same year, Dr. Gills was appointed by Governor Jeb Bush to the Board of Directors of the Florida Sports Foundation. In 2004 Dr. Gills was invited to join the prestigious Florida Council of 100, an advisory committee reporting directly to the governor on various aspects of Florida public policy affecting the quality of life and economic well-being of all Floridians.

While Dr. Gills has many accomplishments and varied interests, his primary focus is to restore physical vision to patients and bring spiritual enlightenment through his life. Guided by his strong and enduring faith in Jesus Christ, he seeks to encourage and comfort the patients who come to St. Luke's and to share his faith whenever possible. It was through sharing his insights with patients that he initially began writing on Christian topics. An avid student of the Bible for many years, he now has authored seventeen books on Christian living, with over five million in print. With the exception of the Bible, Dr. Gills' books are the most widely requested books in the U.S. prison system. In addition, Dr. Gills has published more than 185 medical articles and authored or coauthored nine medical reference textbooks. Five of those books were best-sellers at the American Academy of Ophthalmology annual meetings.

As an ultra-distance athlete, Dr. Gills participated in forty-six marathons, including eighteen Boston Marathons and fourteen 100-mile mountain runs. In addition, he completed five Ironman Triathlons in Hawaii and six Double Iron Triathlons. Dr. Gills has served on the National Board of Directors of the Fellowship of Christian Athletes and in 1991 was the first recipient of their Tom Landry Award.

Married in 1962, Dr. Gills and his wife, Heather, have raised two children, Shea and Pit. Shea Gills Grundy, a former attorney now full-time mom, is a graduate of Vanderbilt University and Emory University Law School. She and husband Shane Grundy, M.D. presented the Gills with their first grandchildren—twins, Maggie and Braddock.

They have since been joined by Jimmy Gills and Lily Grace. The Gills' son, J. Pit Gills, M.D., ophthalmologist, received his medical degree from Duke University Medical Center and in 2001 joined the St. Luke's staff. "Dr. Pit" and his wife, Joy, are the proud parents of Pitzer and Parker.

DID YOU ENJOY THIS BOOK?

Dr. and Mrs. James P. Gills would love to hear from you! Please let them know if *Love: Fulfilling the Ultimate Quest* has had an effect in your life or in the lives of your loved ones. Send your letters to:

St. Luke's Cataract and Laser Institute
P.O. Box 5000
Tarpon Springs, FL 34688-5000
Telephone: (727) 938-2020, Ext. 2200
      (800) 282-9905, Ext. 2200
Fax: (727) 372-3605
Website: www.lovepress.com

OTHER MATERIALS
BY JAMES P. GILLS, M.D.

DARWINISM UNDER THE MICROSCOPE: HOW RECENT SCIEN-
TIFIC EVIDENCE POINTS TO DIVINE DESIGN
(coauthored with Tom Woodward, Ph.D.)
Read about the truth of Creation that your science texts have been avoiding.
ISBN 0-88419-925-8

GOD'S PRESCRIPTION FOR HEALING: FIVE DIVINE GIFTS OF
HEALING
Grow in wonder and appreciation of God as you read about His five divine
gifts of healing to us.
ISBN 1-59185-286-2

IMAGINATIONS: MORE THAN YOU THINK
This book shows how focusing our thoughts will help us grow closer to God.
ISBN 1-59185-609-4

RX FOR WORRY: A THANKFUL HEART
Dr. Gills shows how each of us can find peace by resting and rejoicing in the
promises of God.
ISBN 0-88419-932-0

SPIRITUAL BLINDNESS: DEPENDING ON GOD, ABIDING IN
TRUE FAITH
Jesus + anything = nothing. Jesus + nothing = everything. Here is a book that
will help you recognize the spiritual blindness in all of us and fulfill the
Lord's plan for you.
ISBN 1-59185-607-8

THE DYNAMICS OF WORSHIP: LOVING GOD THROUGH
GENUINE WORSHIP
Designed to rekindle the heart with a passionate love for God, it gives the
who, what, when, where, why, and how of worship.
ISBN 1-59185-657-4

THE PRAYERFUL SPIRIT: PASSION FOR GOD, COMPASSION FOR
PEOPLE
This book tells how prayer has changed Dr. Gills' life, as well as the lives of
patients and other doctors.
ISBN 1-59185-215-3

COME UNTO ME: GOD'S CALL TO INTIMACY
Inspired by Dr. Gills' trip to the Holy Land, it explores God's eternal desire for mankind to get to know Him intimately.

ISBN 1-59185-214-5

TEMPLE MAINTENANCE: EXCELLENCE WITH LOVE
A how-to book for achieving lifelong total fitness of body, mind, and spirit.

ISBN 1-879938-01-4

BELIEVE AND REJOICE: CHANGED BY FAITH, FILLED WITH JOY
This book explores how faith in God can let us see His heart of joy.

ISBN 1-59185-608-6

THE UNSEEN ESSENTIAL: A STORY FOR OUR TROUBLED TIMES
A compelling, contemporary novel about one man's struggle to grow into God's kind of love.

ISBN 1-879938-05-7

TENDER JOURNEY: A CONTINUING STORY FOR OUR TROUBLED TIMES
The popular sequel to *The Unseen Essential.*

ISBN 1-879938-17-0

A BIBLICAL ECONOMICS MANIFESTO: ECONOMICS AND THE CHRISTIAN WORLDVIEW
(coauthored with Ronald H. Nash, Ph.D.)
Money and economics are necessities of life; read what the Bible has to say about them.

ISBN 0-88419-871-5

THE WORRY DISEASE
A colorful 4- by 8.5-inch pamphlet on the most common disease.

TRANSFORM YOUR MARRIAGE
An elegant 4- by 8.5-inch booklet to help couples develop new closeness with each other and with the Lord.

ISBN 1-879938-11-1